THE

INDIAN MUSE

IN

ENGLISH GARB

THE

INDIAN MUSE

IN

ENGLISH GARB

BEHRAMJI MERWANJI MALABARI

GYAN

Published by

GYAN

Gyan Publishing House
5, Ansari Road
Daryaganj, New Delhi-110002
Phone: 011-47034999, 9811692060
E-mail: books@gyanbooks.com

Distribution Network
gyanbooks.com
India, USA, Canada, UK, Australia

ISBN: 978-93-7097-475-3 (PB)

First Published, 1876

2nd Impression 2025

Printed at: Gyan Press, Delhi.

THE INDIAN MUSE IN ENGLISH GARB
Arthur BEHRAMJI MERWANJI MALABARI

THE

INDIAN MUSE

IN

ENGLISH GARB.

BY

BEHRAMJI MERWANJI MALABARI,

AUTHOR OF

NITI-VINOD

OR

PLEASURES OF MORALITY.

1876.

To

MISS MARY CARPENTER,

RED LODGE HOUSE, BRISTOL.

MADAM,

It is close upon a year, since I obtained your kind permission to dedictae my English verses to you. I do it now with mingled feelings of pride and pleasure. If I did not do so before, it was because of my desire to make it presentable to a lady of your wide sympathies—one who has made such glad sacrifices for her sisters of India. The harvest of your labour of love, Madam, dwells in your own heart: my utmost effort has been to strew that heart with a string of feeble songs. But such as it is, you are most welcome to it; and to all that a grateful heart can feel for the well-wisher of his country.

Yours, Madam,

With respectful admiration,

B. M. MALABARI.

CONTENTS.

PREFACE.

The writer of these lines commenced the study of English, about eleven years ago, under very trying circumstances—want of means and of clever, conscientious teachers. With the latter difficulty, he struggled on for about two years and a half; and then with almost a self-acquired knowledge of the elements, joined the Surat Mission School, under the superintendence of the late Rev. William Dixon, a very worthy gentleman from Belfast, and a scholar of brilliant promise. It was here, that some time after, the author began to attract notice by his predilection for English literature. Though he belonged to a lower class, special arrangements were made for him to join his seniors, whenever a lecture on Shakspeare was expected; and as a return for the concession, he was required to explain the more difficult lines to those who could not follow the lecturer. It was very flattering, indeed, to an Indian of fourteen summers, to interpret lines of the Myriad-minded to men double his age; but he suspects his pupils spared the poor boy any very searching tests; or that, perhaps Heaven had spared those gentlemen the inconvenience of a critical or appreciative taste.

After a course of two years and six months here, the author was found qualified to present himself at the University Entrance Examination. And here ceased all the systematic education of which he can boast. His pride too was effectually humbled at this stage. Three times he failed at the Examination; and scraped through it the fourth time, by the barest chance. The reason, though not far to seek, need not be disclosed here, as it hardly interests the readers.

In his own way, however, the author was not idle all this while. He has devoured, he believes, more poetry in one year than he could digest in five. Many of the British poets, Shakspeare, Byron, Shelley, Burns, Wordsworth, Keats and Campbell in particular, have long become his household gods. He worships them with a strong, passionate heart-homage, and derives the chief happiness of life from them. Such a taste could not long remain without its effects. At eighteen he felt an irresistible desire to make verses Acting upon the impulse, he multiplied lines upon lines, till in 1872, they grew to nearly five thousand. These lines were much liked by several competent judges, among the earliest of them, the Hon. Sorabji Shapurji Bengali, Rev. J. V. S. Taylor, Messsr. Mansukhram Suryaram, Ranchhodbhai Udairam, and last but most, by the late Dr. Wilson; and mainly through the exertions of this good and great man, two successive editions were taken out in a short time. This book was written in pure Gujaráti, Gujaráti racy of the soil—a feat attempted by few and achieved by fewer Parsis. The Doctor was charmed with its success; and in a moment of generous pride, asked the author why he could not present H. R. H. the Prince of Wales, on the happy occasion of his visit to Bombay, with a few English verses. The idea took, and in a few weeks about six hundred lines were submitted to Dr. Wilson, who spoke very kindly of them, and held out high hopes of seeing them accepted by the illustrious Visitor.

Time wore on; and the Bombayites at last set their anxious eyes on their future Emperor. But in the midst of the general rejoicings that followed, not a few hearts were overcast with deep anxiety. Dr. Wilson, their venerated friend, was relapsing into a state of exhaustion, from which he had but lately rallied. In a few days, Bombay lost its oldest and best friend—Dr. Wilson died, and with him died the author's hopes of winning the smiles of Royalty! He however remained loyal to his friend's advice, and respectfully applied to the Prince, for permission to present the verses to him. But H. R. H. 'regretted that he was unable to break through the rule he had made of never giving any special permission for the dedication to him, of works, with the authors of which he was not personally acquainted'. Poor ill-starred verses! The timid offspring of a hopeful muse! To be thus treated by him for whom they were so joyously hastened into existence! But the author took heart of grace; and set about thinking what was the next best thing to do. He heard that Miss Carpenter, the zealous advocate of female education in India, was then in Bombay. To apply to her for permission, and to obtain it readily, was the work of a few hours. Such is the history of 'The Indian Muse' and its Indian author. It is more than nine months since then, and the lines have, during the interval, grown almost threefold. The merit of the work is as modest as its scope is limited. It can claim litttle more than a passing interest. This much, the author flatters himself, he can count upon from his own countrymen: in what light the Englishman takes it, he cannot tell. To an observant mind it can not be a secret, that English, which bids fair, at no distant date, to become a world language, has so far identified herself with our dearest interests, that we not only speak and write through her medium : we have grown almost to thinking in English. Persian and Sanskrit are studied for pleasure or for fame ; but the one is too light and the other too heavy for this utilitarian age.

It is English that is becoming the current language of India—the soft insinuating English—rich in her song and her science and her philosophy—the mother and moulder of the divinest human thoughts! We resort to her not only from the selfish political point of view, but from the social and intellectual point. We have schools and colleges enough to rear the rising generation of all Asia; and week by week, the English have been sending us the freshest 'thought-crystals' of the West, in the form of books and reviews and pamphlets. Surely, then, it is no fault of ours if we turn these blessings to some account! It is in this spirit that the author would have his verses viewed by the Englishman : everything else he would leave to his candour.

While the lines were in the compositor's hands, the author was advised to avoid all obscurity attending the metrical compositions of a foreigner. He has, therefore, scattered a few explanatory and other notes here and there, very hastily jotted, for which he craves the reader's indulgence. Though aware of the necessity of an Englishman to examine the proof-sheets, the author has even that satisfaction denied him. Perhaps it is for the best; for the reader will thus be able to see the lines in their beauties and their blemishes.

The author owes one more apology to his readers. For reasons, which it were an insult to them to offer here, he had to be his own scribe and his own proof-reader. It can be easily imagined how glibly the sheets were run over, and how in consequence, some errors in spelling, overlooked. Those already detected are :—

Martial for Marital

and Embroy for Embryo.

Bombay, December 15, 1876.

B. M. M.

An Humble Request.

Thou great and Heav'n-directed Sovereign!
Whose sacred gifts her sex's worth maintain—
Whose holy life bright angels look upon,
As the long Hereafter's clear and hopeful dawn—
Whose noble deeds, in suff'ring hearts embalm'd,
Infix'd remain, with life eternal arm'd—
Whose rule benign reminds th' historic sage,
Of kindred spirits in earth's golden age—
Whom Faith and Genius on the throne surround,
Each hour improving with fresh laurels crown'd—
Whose studious mind, in Care's continuous chains,
Is oft enliven'd by th' inspir'd strains
Of the chaste and graceful Tennysonian muse—
Wouldst thou, great Queen! my homely page peruse?
If pray'r prove aught, let all my pray'rs conjure
One smile benignant on my verse obscure!
And may its light, by time intensifi'd,
Thro' toils and trials be my faithful guide!

And may its warmth to me fresh vigour send;
And both combin'd, a charm to labour lend!
Till modest merit may rejoice a while,
In the glad possession of bright Virtue's smile!

An Address.

Sun of India! pour thy light,
On time-honor'd Delhi's site;
Now revives thy country's right
And changes all her destiny!

Delhi! raise thy humbl'd head,
From a vanquish'd hero's bed;
And behold thy brows o'er-spread
With wreaths of smiling Victory!

There behold the Rajput spear,
And the Moslem scimiter;
With the Highland halberdier
Adorning yon dread cavalry!

See ! how lordly Nizam glares !
Holkar, Scindia and Benares,
Cashmire, Jepur and their heirs
    Evincing all their loyalty !

See the gallant Gaicowar,
Princes of old Katyawar,
And each dominant Durbar
    Increasing thy hilarity !

With bright gems that shame the sun,
And with many a sword and gun,
Thy proud breast they over-run—
    A free and titl'd Yeomanry !

Nobly Lytton play the host !
That's to be thy cherish'd boast ;
And thro' Reuter wire the toast,
    Thou triumph-girted Disraeli !

Welcome ye who're fair and leal,
To this roistering wassail ;
And to every gay detail
    Of universal jubilee !

Claps and cannons roar aloud,
Till you reach yon smiling cloud,
Where the planets silver-brow'd
May imitate your heraldry!

Delhi! kneel, in joy serene,
To thy glorious Empress-queen;
And exultant chant the pean
Of pure and life-long fealty!

Sun of Heaven! pour thy light,*
From that proud cerulean height,
On the Crown divinely bright
Of Her Imperial Majesty!

The Welcome.

Ye India's sons and daughters all, who health and plenty share,
Prepare yourselves to welcome here, Britannia's son and heir.

* The first three lines here are each a syllable shorter than in Campbell's Hohenlinden. I should be sorry if this offends the English ear. But a short pause after the first syllable, somehow makes the whole look more like an *address*.

To her, for sacrifices grave, a heavy debt remains,
For countless British heroes' blood has fed old India's veins.
The sun of India's glory once revolv'd with light intense,
And glad the human soul imbib'd her genial vigour thence.
When wave-conceal'd and barren lay the distant British isle,
Our glorious land enjoy'd the warmth of God's inspiring smile.
Her classic arts rejoicing earn'd high Heav'n's approval seal,
Her stately science markéd srokes of genius did reveal.
Her flora, to the mind diseas'd, sweet thrills of pleasure sent,
And Nature musick'd on, in dulcet tones of keen content.
Time was when Indian genius beam'd resplendent and sublime,
But now the eye, in vain, looks for the traces of that time.

Ere civil horrors hardly yet had left her rich domain,
And blows, with deadly aims exchang'd, had hardly ceas'd to rain;
When Tartars, Afgans and Moguls, by grim Islam sustain'd,
Engag'd the patriot Rajputs brave, to life austere train'd;
When giant Sikhs, with firmness mute, destroy'd and bled by turn;
And nomad Marathas revolts infus'd with unconcern;
When native strength, no longer, could with safety hold its own,
And friends and allies' faith was with dead apathy o'er-grown;
The squat phlegmatic Dutchman came, prepar'd with efforts grand,
To furnish with rich Indian spoils his pigmy father-land.
With nervous rueful twitches sore, he kept his countenance,
And with spasmodic bursts of sense heroic did penance.

Till when this Holland's hero-bird, stripp'd of his warrior-wing,
Sank placidly into his forte of thrifty trafficking.
Then wolves of frozen West, pour'd in the hungry Portuguese,
With India's dainties rich and rare, their cravings to appease.
Distorting long the genius of a pure and righteous faith,
With Persecution's tainted tongue, they poison'd Virtue's breath.
Now came the Frenchman vain, supreme in selfishness polite,
With India's remnant blood, to glut his beggar appetite.
To feeling lost, his harden'd heart no scruple could endure—
A blending mixture of the atheist and the epicure!
In indecisive balance trembled then the life of man,
When vice and crime, intoxicate with power, rampant ran.

It seem'd as if the King of kings look'd on in carelessness,
And to the millions woe-begone would never give redress.
Till sin accumulated form'd a system infinite,
Of foul corruption social and of ethical conceit.
But soon it tott'ring stood, before the gaze divine, evolv'd,
In whose indignant glare it was entirely dissolv'd.
And now a nation rose to power and to glory bright,
To represent the light of Heav'n, found fit in Heaven's sight.
The Lord's elect, successive they inherit and bequeath
The maiden's crown of virtue and the patriot's laurel wreath.
And here this Prince, their idol comes, wean'd from their warm embrace,
With graciousness to cheer the hearts of India's mixéd race.
Whose hopeless illness once your souls did with suspense invest,

Whose wondrous cure your bated breath restor'd, is
now your guest.
Recall the day when Death besieg'd the portals of
his life,
When Life and Death were fast engag'd in close and
mortal strife.
When on Eternity's dread floods, th' unconscious
patient hung,
And woe-oppresséd hearts were by suspense and an-
guish wrung.
When but the oil of Faith could feed, afresh, the
lamp of Hope,
And constant Love and pure alone, with sullen Death
could cope.
Remember him whose fate provok'd remote and alien
souls,
To prayers joint, effectual made by sacred temple-
tolls. *
The presence of that soul reviv'd, has sanctified our
shore;

* So thinks the honest Hindu.

Now blended blessings still unknown, will blossom
more and more.
Shake off the rust of coldness then, and wear the
gown of grace;
And hail with cheers this advent bright which all your
pains repays.
Ye Indian Chiefs and Princes brave, who loyalty pro-
fess,
With splendid welcome and sincere, the royal mind
impress.
The scion of a gen'rous race, by Heav'n to India's
lent,
Old India's might and glory then, ye fairly represent.
And all ye fortune's friends! this great event immortal-
ize;
And for remembrance safe, your means abundant
exercise.
And now ye sons of Mercury! your loyalty evince,
And prove to this illustrious Prince, you too are each
a prince.
Let Wealth and Will go hand in hand, two close and
mutual friends,

And for the lack of former, by the latter make amends.
Let Nature's smiling beauties, and the trophies of your art,
Keen joy in blended sweetness, to the royal mind impart.
Let India's sun of Learning bright in grandeur slow arise,
And dazzle with his vari'd rays, the noble stranger's eyes.
Let all his wishes, yet unborn, anticipated be,
And let his glad surprise for their response, be all your fee.
That when the voice of Novelty his travel's record hails,
He may with pride and joy recite what comfort here prevails.
Then let your wish to God ascend, thro' Pray'rs effectual door,
That He, this sacred pledge, may soon to anxious arms, restore.

With breath suspended o'er the seas, a heart maternal
waits,
Which fanci'd risk, by absence bred, with throbs of
pain vibrates.
A trust-bound soul's emotions can no settl'd shape
assume,
By Hope and Fear alternate urg'd, for rest she finds
no room.
Then loud ye sturdy sons of India, raise your manly
voice,
And with your suit sincere to Heav'n, two troubl'd
hearts rejoice.
And Indias' daughters ye, your voice with winning
grace equip,
For sweet is Pray'r and grateful, breath'd by modest
virgin-lips!

"The dream of my youth" H. R. H. the Prince of Wales.

I dreamt a grateful dream,
Nor heavy nor uncouth,
When life's unsettl'd stream
Scarce met the waves of youth.

I dreamt a cradle high,
With rich surroundings free;
Its head protected by
Th' etherial canopy.

Its noble pillars bright
Were pure and solid gold;
Their straight and soaring height
Spoke majesty untold.

Its graceful form, the frame,
To stately cedar ow'd;
And stones of deathless flame,
Were on its sides bestow'd.

And from the China worm
It took its silk supply;
And faithful she and firm,
Did naught for use deny.

Its folds were fill'd anon,
With breaths of fragrance choice;
Whose soothing power won
My soul to lasting joys.

The portraits round it cast,
Were splendid tho' grotesque;
In effect, they surpast
The quaint and picturesque!

And from the land of dreams,
My roving mind tho' turn'd;
But still my mem'ry's gleams,
In all their freshness burn'd.

I woke, and strange to see,
Unlike such scenes surmis'd,
In all fidelity,
My dream was realiz'd! *

The cradle is the land
Of glorious Hindustan,
Whose sketches midst I stand,
Though now a full-grown man!

And all the sights I saw,
No empty shadows were;
Then undefin'd and raw,
They now with motion stir!

This wondrous land is mine,
And all its fertile banks;
For this Thy gift divine,
O Lord! I give Thee thanks.

* Yes; realized and perhaps more than realized. But I wonder if less august personages see *their* dreams thus come true: for human nature, it must be owned, is sadly given to dreaming. I, for instance, sometimes dream that we are to have, in God's good time, a certain little Prince of the Blood Royal as our own Emperor, to live in the midst of us, and have an *Indian* parliament, with *Indian* Legislative and Executive Officers. But then it is *my* dream!

A Message sent with H. R. H. the Prince of Wales.

'Tell Mamma we are happy' * here,
Amidst her mercy's flow ;
That still we have a smile or tear,
To share her weal or woe—

No starts of rude surprise dispel
Our charm of harmony ;
But joint in duty, glad we dwell,
A blessèd family !—

Our dearest wishes hang upon
Her glory and her state ;
To guard these, then, our lives we pawn ;
And for the moment wait,

When in an evil hour, the foe
Our Empress seeks to grieve ;
We'll then all selfish joys forego ;
And then our name retrieve—

* Such were the words, I am told, tastefully rendered in gas, adorning an arch erected at the entrance of the house in which H. H. the Rájá of Rájpiplá was staying, during the visit of H. R. H. the Prince of Wales to Bombay. This quaint device was, no doubt, the spontaneous expression of the Rájá's gratefulness to his Sovereign; and the words following, I am sure, convey the common sentiments of the vast nations of India.

Till then, whene'er our knees we bend,
Our pray'rs to Godward send,
To Him we'll cordially commend
Our Mother, Queen and Friend !

To H. M. S. S. Serapis, when she started for India.

Thou noble ship ! pray nobly bear
Thy Charge to soils remote ;
And ride the sea with constant care,
His safety to promote.

When Dara * and Askandar * plough'd
The waves with energy,
Their ships were not so well endow'd
To grace the solemn Sea.

No such spontaneous welcome cheer'd
Their proud and precious freights,
As now, by close approach endear'd,
Thy gracious lord awaits.

* Darius of Persia and Alexander of Macedon, the earliest invaders of India, and each the *beau ideal* of Oriental sovereigns.

No Hope so earnest ever dwelt,
In such a frail abode;
And never Trust with fear unfelt,
Such doubtful regions trode.

From greater strength, then we expect
More faithful work and strong;
So safety with thy speed connect,
And faith with service long.

Then calmly march the main; and swift
With conscious pow'r proceed;
And those who welcome's hand uplift,
Will offer thee God-speed!

True in life and in death.*

Albert! to holy keeping though consign'd,
By friendly hearts and kindred, left behind;

* The death of the Prince Consort was not merely a personal or a national loss; it was a loss universal. And as such it was felt in India. I remember its effects to this day, though then I was but a child. The news flashed upon us with all the violence of a *calamity*. The English must have naturally felt the blow nearer their hearts. But who can conceive the soul-struggles of the bereaved wife? They would beggar all surmises. The world since then, has been a blank to her, for all the show of sunshine her rank imposes on her. Life, for her ceased to live with the death of him who had grown to be the very 'mainstay of life.' But though shrinking from all contact with the world, she has not shrunk from her duty—that of tending their offspring—*hers* and *his*. May the light of their blended love guide the steps of their dear ones; and may the united memory of the Royal cousin-lovers endure for ever and ever!

Though years sad and long, the page have seal'd
Of Book so holy bright, so short reveal'd;
Though nations wept aloud, and desperate
With heart-felt grief, discuss'd their future fate;
Though British hearts and hearths a prospect wore,
Of sanguine grief and touching pity sore;
Thou'st left *one* soul, whose depth is passing deep;
Whose nature—soft—believing, cannot keep
Afar thy image, deep-impress'd on soil
Sō yielding. Far from joy, with anguish'd toil,
A bleeding heart, a spirit panting clings
To thee! Asleep, awake, thy thought rebrings
Her love—absorbing and eternal love,
That breathes below to breathe in thee above!
A soul whom joy nor grief from thee can wean:
That soul's thy light, thy life, thy wife, thy queen!
Whose solace sole is the remembrance dear,
Of sweets domestic, drunk for many a year.
Whose spirit oft to realms etherial swells,
Where rich in joys, her saintly idol dwells.

If scenes invite her sense, they cost a glance

Of meaning anguish, and recall perchance
The Past ; so lately pass'd, so fatal pure :
A shadow comes ; and then—can she be sure ?
Can that benign and stately form that floats
Upon her sight ; on which with rapture dotes
Her wistful soul—Those calm seraphic eyes,
A look at which her yearning satisfies—
That heav'nly presence which a glory casts
Around, of joy that all her grief outlasts—
Can these, that glad in her the wife arouse,
These vivid signs, be of her sainted spouse ?
Fain would she her believing heart obey ;
But cruel Past dispells the welcome ray
Of Hope ; and then the heart, its wound to hide,
Seeks fanci'd joys ; the while too sorely tried
By Sorrow, jealous of his gloomy reign ;
Who yokes her spirit to a life-long pain !
Yet still, each thought, a lasting charity,
From self remov'd, her self from pain makes free.
Her days, though dragg'd with pain, are oft reliev'd
By love for her maternal worth conceiv'd.
And cheer'd by Hope, with sweet Reunion's gleam,
She lives amidst her nations' proud esteem !

To the Memory of one of the Noblest friends of India.*

O tell me why those briny pearls
Are trembling in yon widow's eyes ?
And why her guileless orphan girls,
Thus break their hearts with echoing sighs ?
What's it the holy man with awe,
In accents tremulous relates ?
At which the list'ners' bosoms thaw,
Which thrilling on their souls vibrates !
And how's it, on Malabar cliff,*
Which usual lives in bustle great,
That people treading slow and stiff,
In whispers low ejaculate ?
And why that man, oppress'd with age,
In anguish mute his forehead beats ?
As slowly from the Guardian's * page,
His dim and tear-stain'd sight retreats ;

* The Rev. Dr. John Wilson, too well known to need any poetic tribute. His life was living poetry and his work a soul-song !

* The residence of the late worthy.

* A Christian weekly, much read by those who seek spiritual rather than social news.

And whence that proud assemblage here,
Of Pow'r and Wealth and Virtue brave?
And whence that loud convulsive tear,
That grateful wets a fresh-made grave!

What means that solemn cortege there?
Where Prince and Peasant mingle tears;
Where many a spirit stout and fair,
Thus clinging to that grave appears!

What then, has Wilson's dove-like soul,
For saints' abode, her pinions spread?
And do his *bones*, so near their goal,
Enjoy this pageant and parade?

What sterling worth that soul's must be!
How deep with genius rare imbu'd!
Nor Friendship, Love nor Poetry
Can measure such a magnitude!

Few lives have such a lustre shed,
On human soul, in modern days,
As he th' evangelistic head,
On poor benighted Indian race.

Few minds on Asian lore could turn,
With such a wondrous native bent;
Few tastes thus happily discern
The treasures of the Orient.

Few hearts were so unselfish spent,
In sympathy appropriate,
As his and of that graceful saint—
His soul-adopted Margaret! *

How like a shepherd, kind and free,
He hous'd and help'd the sick and poor!
Till Grief, and Want and Misery,
For solace sought his magic door!
Now as he wins his Lord's esteem,
His honours angels' hearts engage;
And saints in Heaven envy him
His patriarchal pilgrimage!

---

* Margaret Bayne, Dr. Wilson's first wife. The saying 'Marriages are made in Heaven' strikes me very forcibly whenever I read this lady's memoirs published by her husband. She seems to have been, in every way, a wife worthy of such a man. All sympathy and all sentiment, she gladly sacrificed her precious young life in doing good. Her loss to *him*, it would be a sacrilege to estimate!

A dying man to his Soul*

My soul ! why flutt'rest thou so oft ?
Why breaks thy march serene ?
When Death, the reaper turneth soft,
To reap the hire of sin.

Why faintest thou in sore dismay ?
My nervous, timid soul !
If Death dissolves this 'coil of clay,'
The grave is not *thy* goal !

Why sweat'st so ? soul ! why such a gloom
From Death's approach derive ?
When thou'lt at last, in all thy bloom,
The death of Death survive !

Oh still, be still thou tim'rous soul !
And wing thy way above,
When angels ring the parting knoll ;
To meet the Lord of Love !

* These lines were suggested to me, while once reading to Dr. Wilson, during his last illness, some verses of the Royal Psalmist and some of Heber's beautiful lines, of which the Doctor was very fond.

The Stages of a Hindu Female Life.

In Kachh * I saw the light of Heav'n: a sad and dreary day
The first of my existence was, from welcome far away.
My baby-mother paid too dear, for one who could not bail
Her sad devoted life, from ills that motherhood assail.
Her infant years had trac'd their course thro' sad and harrowing scenes,
And fresh afflictions greeted her, before she reach'd her teens.
Long ere the light of womanhood upon her soul had dawn'd,
Her hopeful life was basely to precarious future pawn'd.
A dry and lack-love man of four and fifty was her spouse,
And she of tender ten, when urg'd, she took the nuptial vows!

* Once the hot-bed of the frightful social crime, female infanticide.

A self-imposèd duty taught her visions to conjure,
In whose delusive lull, she sold her heart to lust impure.
Now all the mock solemnities and heartless pageants o'er,
The spell-bound spirit starts with fear th' excitement hid before.
Scarce wean'd from happy infancy, her dream of life undreamt,
From all contaminating thoughts, her mind was yet exempt.
Awe-struck and mute, foul custom's prey, she strove to face the change ;
But nature ever faithful, self from self could not enstrange.
And love, of his approach her soul had hardly yet appriz'd,
When bitter duty, through her wife's estate, she realiz'd.
Those hallow'd extacies and joys, divinely sanctified,

Which heart to heart unite, were to this hapless pair
denied.
Those sanction'd sweets that render life deserving of a
trial,
Of these, the ill-match'd lives had e'er to take a cold
denial

* * * *

Time shook his magic wand and smooth'd the serious
gap of age,
Th' unhappy girl now felt advancing towards maternal
stage.
And proud and fond my sire caress'd his strangely
wedded ward,
And breath'd a selfish pray'r to Heav'en his coming
heir to guard!
And tho' my martyr-mother cross'd the stage with
crucial throes,
The frightful task upon her did the stamp of death
impose.
Though God in mercy did not like her wreckèd life
to save,

To soothe my selfish sire, reclaim'd me from a fleshy
grave.
More dead than live the mourning friends in pity
carried me,
To him who anxious stood to take his dead love's
legacy.
My sire gave a mingl'd look of grief and joy intense,
And then his pent up feelings with a burst unhing'd
his sense.
For days and nights he raving pass'd a fearful strug-
gle through,
Till soft the 'peace of hope' crept up his troubl'd
mental view.
But soon the tide of time effac'd each vestige of his
pain;
His loss he now made light of, as he gloated on his
gain.
His love to her he lost, was but a means to end devis'd;
What reck'd he for the means, now that his end was
realiz'd?
Thus early doom'd was I, to lose the tenderest of kin;

Unconscious of the ruin I wrought, so strangely
usher'd in !
The joy a first-born e'er creates in fond maternal
heart—
The welcome glimpse of hope, at which her pulses
swifter start—
The shrinking glance with which she meets the husband's fondest gaze—
The boundless faith in future which her mortal fears
allays—
The smile triumphant which her look in chasten'd love
arrays—
While with the gift instinct, her lord's anxiety she
repays—
These soft emotions which her life to anguish reconcile,
Such anguish as no joys but those of motherhood beguile—
These thrills, my mother felt not, nor that glad triumphant glance

Adorn'd her face, now wrapt in pale repose of deadly
trance.
And thus, a stranger's breast retain'd in me the passing
breath;
And for a world of woes, reserv'd me, from a happy
death.
My infant years sped in bliss serene, that knew no
bound;
For both the parents' love and care, I in my sire
found.
But thro' a female heir, his hope of Swarg, * he said,
was scant;
So urg'd by fate, a stranger now he let his girl sup-
plant.!
And with the remnant of his age, as if, to temporize,
He launch'd himself, once more, upon a martial enter-
prize!
Though turn'd of three score six, he brought a second
baby bride,
In age and size and female grace, a pigmy at my side!

* The place where the Hindu's soul finds final rest.

For youth and health spontaneous had in me their
charms combin'd,
And there I stood in Asian bloom most gorgeous and
refin'd.
Now conscious of the fact, at once, my sire took alarm.
And studiously he sought, he said, 'to keep me out of
harm'!
A sickly boy of twelve he found to take me off his
hand,
As guardian of my honour and as husband to command!
My soul at first revolted at a union so uncouth—
I long'd to live in answ'ring love, impell'd by sanguine
youth.
But false I could not be to him, whose fault I saw
was none;
So with a trust in time, on self, a victory I won.
And time was true as e'er, and soon my soul-felt want
supplied;
And flush'd with mellow manhood, stood my lord in
manhood's pride!

My melted soul in music waves, towards him began to
flow;
For Love's the steward faithful of true happiness below.
And he, my lord, my patience long, as if to recompense,
Ador'd me with a passion, oh! so lasting, so intense!
Thus soul in soul dissolv'd, we drank our fill of wedded joy;
Our lives a live-long rapture which e'en sameness could
not cloy!
But short-liv'd was the raptur'd dream, now loathsome
for its glare;
It vanish'd, leaving to my sight, its shadow pale and
bare.
Secure in nuptial calm, when least the shoals of life
I fear'd,
My love was wreck'd upon a rock which sudden there
appear'd.
Content not with my sire's love, his young unhappy
spouse,

Had e'er so long been trifling with my husband's sacred vows!
To keep me off my guard he play'd so cleverly his role,
That ere my doubts found being, he with guilt had stain'd his soul.
One windy night, a hedious cry my fitful slumbers broke;
And quick my father dragg'd me out of bed before I woke.
His wither'd frame was writhing sore, in passion's agony:
His eyes exhal'd the sparks subdued of sated jealousy.
He pointed at his room, wherein, I rush'd with bodings rife:
I saw my hapless spouse beside my father's second wife!
Too true my doubts; that night he was the lawless woman's guest;
And dreadful was the fate that reach'd this violent incest!

My sire had, in a frenzied fit, surpris'd the guilty
pair;
And with a vengeful blade despatch'd my husband
then and there!
The siren he reserv'd for fate proportionately fell;
But ere he could the threat perform he saw the mur-
d'rer's cell!
Though great the wrong he bore, the world *his* outrage
could not bear:
And ere a month elaps'd, he had his victim's fate to
share.
An orphan and a widow! oh what thrills that thought
inspires!
Made orphan by a husband's hand, and widow by a
sire's!

Nature Triumphant over caste.

A piteous cry of woe escap'd
A wee untended child;
The listless rabble idly gap'd,
Or mercilessly smil'd.

The heated sun block'd up his breath ;
And now midst groanings deep,
Unconscious of approaching death,
He sobb'd himself to sleep.

Thick grows the breathing of the child ;
His limbs in anguish writhe ;
Once full of animation wild,
So light, so free, and lithe !

No heart the waif deserted, mov'd,
Though death remain'd not far ;
For by his fated looks, he prov'd
The offspring of a Mhar *

No, none could touch a thing so vile ;
None so devoid of self ;
Thus would have died the poor exile,
But for some timely help.

A Hindu widow eyed the scene,
Herself a mother young ;
His speechless woe, full well I ween,
Her heart with pity wrung.

* A very low caste Hindu.

And tho' she long'd to render aid,
It was to her denied;
A dry disease, of sorrow bred,
Her sacred milk had dried.

With melting eyes she clutch'd the bairn;
And yielding him her breast,
For pow'r, for which her heart did yearn,
Her glance to Heav'n addrest.

When, joy of joys, her pray'r ascends,
Of tender mercy born,
To Him Who mercy e'er extends,
Its practice to adorn!

The matron's breast, the Lord supplies,
With fresh vivific stores;
Though gain'd with bitter sacrifice,
There's none that gift ignores.

The lookers-on astonish'd stand;
This act their feelings hurts;
But nature, by divine command,
Her power now asserts.

That moment, in sweet mercy's waves,
They drown the demon Caste;
And as their looks of ire she braves,
They quite forgive the past!

Where indeed?

'Men of England,' Campbell.

Men of India! Where's your valiance?
Matrons! where's your spirit free?
Maidens! where's your modest presence?
Youths! where is your chivalry?

Men! how envi'd were your fathers,
For their wonted bravery?
Now your country scarcely gathers
E'en a steady soldiery!

Patriots, poets, who can bring them?
Artists! where's your mastery?
Foeman's dangers, who's to sing them?
Who's to lead th' artillery?

Matrons! where's your blind allegiance?
Where's your boasted chastity?
Where's that noble gift religion's—
Patience in adversity?

Maidens ! where's your love romantic ?
Unprofan'd by perjury ;
Love, that by its fervence frantic,
Lends to life a witchery !

Youths ! ye hopes of generations,
Whence your moral slavery ?
Of the once proud Aryan nations,
Ye inglorious mockery !

India, thus her fame o'er-shading,
Steeps herself in misery ;
While her glorious past is fading,
From fair Hist'ry's memory !

A life of trouble.

The storm-begotten wind convuls'd
The agèd hillock's side ;
What time the elements repuls'd
The hunted felon's bride.

An angry night was that, and bleak,
Unconscious when she slept ;
When loud the wind his rage did wreak ;
And captive nature wept.

A blissful infancy was hers,
In wanton freedom spent;
Her parents knew no Sorrow's curse;
They knew so well Content.

But Death, the chast'ner of the soul,
A visit to them paid;
The wife, obedient to his roll,
Was gather'd to the dead.

And from her close but cold embrace,
The sire took his child;
In after days she saw no trace
Of his despair so wild.

And there she liv'd a fairy free,
His heart's asylum nigh;
His fondest dream's design was she,
On earth his only tie.

Her youth assum'd a mellow grace;
Care stood not on her brow;
And on her sweet seraphic face,
Her soul divine did glow.

Th' enraptur'd sun, with tribute rays,
Her beauty sought to bribe;
And on her accents, Music's preys,
Thick grew the warbling tribe.

An ardent youth, whose soul was sear'd
With Lust's consuming sin,
Her cousin he, with hopes appear'd
Her virgin heart to win.

His frantic court and wild appeal,
Abruptly rous'd the maid,
From dreams of innocence ideal
And feelings chaste and staid.

For ere she knew she had a heart,
Her heart was not her own;
True Love, her nature's counterpart
Had chang'd her nature's tone.

Her love was pledg'd past all recall,
To him who felt full well,
Her fascination's binding thrall,
And glori'd in the spell.

In him her dream was realiz'd,
Her wishes echo'd back;
Her virgin fame was compromis'd,
Impell'd by love's attack.

The cousin saw th' attchment, through
The glass of jealousy;
And the rapture of his love turn'd to
Foul hatred's agony.

He call'd his rival out, to try,
In duel, fortune's run;
When lo! by dint of spirits high,
The favour'd lover won.

The fatal combat's issue dark,
A well-kept secret was,
From her who harmless set the spark—
The bloodshed's hapless cause.

But by misgivings work'd upon,
Her heart was sorely tried;
She felt some awful danger yawn,
To gulp her love affied.

Instinctively she reach'd the spot;
When stripp'd she stood of speech;
Her sight fell on a body shot,
Beyond recov'ry's reach!

Her aim was ta'en, her fear remov'd,
The woman in her stirr'd;
Alive to instant risk, she prov'd
Her sex's will forward.

His safety now her thoughts engross'd,
So madly compromis'd;
She then a hurried flight propos'd
To him she priceless priz'd.

They sought a wind-worn mountain's edge,
Expos'd to wrath divine;
For love she laid her life a pledge,
On love's exacting shrine!

The dark unvari'd solitude,
Upon their courage prey'd;
The faintest rustle in the wood,
To them their doom convey'd!

This could not last; Remorse imbib'd
His blood, with guilt imbu'd;
The culprit thus by law proscrib'd,
By nature was eschew'd.

And when death mark'd him for his own,
Forgetting selfish fear,
With breaking heart, without a groan,
She seal'd her love's career!

Th' intensity of loneliness,
Her anguish'd soul did melt;
Which at the sight of his distress,
She never show'd she felt.

But now the final scene provok'd
A stream of scalding tears,
The flood of which her bosom choak'd:
She'd done with hopes and fears!

But still a duty glad remain'd,
The thought of which, reviv'd,
Her drooping spirit now maintain'd,
Till late of sense depriv'd.

The fruit of their conjugal state,
A quick sanguineous pledge,
Was left her to conciliate
Her life's severe outrage. *

Her fragile frame, unhing'd by care,
Had half its blood destroy'd ;
And now she had e'en that to share,
With one her thoughts employ'd.

Her own existence' lamp burnt pale,
The oil had sunk so low ;
Her state did fresher cares entail ;
And heavier ado.

And still this unknown visitor,
Her way to comfort pa'vd ;
But when she op'd past mem'ry's door,
In frenzi'd grief she rav'd !

* The intelligent reader will at once detect 'outrage' in this line, and one or two other dissylables elsewhere, as instances of misaccentuation. But one is loath to part with an expressive rhyme, for such a reason, especially when he has the authority of almost all standard authors on his side. The writer offers this explanation not out of conceit, but because he would avoid, at all hazards, pleading guilty to any gross ignorance.

That burst of grief, with throes prevail'd,
Which thought can not depinct ;
When safely, pitying Nature hal'd
A babe with life instinct !

In mix'd emotions, sweetly strange,
The mourner now was lost ;
Her dreary life now found a change ;
Though bought at frightful cost.

But not much longer than an hour,
Could she this flower tend ;
For soon alas ! its infant pow'r,
Was seen with death to blend.

And ere Invention's fruitful mind,
Some project could concert,
The mother in her arms did find
A load of flesh inert !

Her sad surrender to her fate
Betrays no anguish-throbs ;
For now her grief disconsolate
Her eyes of tears robs.

With dead activity she takes
Her ill-starr'd offspring's poll;
Then towards her husband's grave she makes,
And opes the hallow'd hole.

And there her dead love's relic still,
With vacant looks she stows,
Upon her lover's bosom chill;
Then *she* too lifeless grows!

Now reading this historiette brief,
The soul to frenzy drives;
In bitterness she thinks as if
Fate wanton'd with these lives!

Ah me! 'tis out of Fancy's ken,
To paint this weird affair;
The chisel pencil or the pen
Must trace its strokes on air.

More sinn'd against than sinning, they
Endur'd a life-long grief;
But joint in death, they'll live and pray
To Him Who gives relief!

Lost Love.

Fly, fly my stricken soul!
My spirit Heav'nward roll;
My Love my fate doth toll;
I've lov'd and lost!

She whom my soul ador'd;
First did me hope accord;
Then left me for the Lord,
In anguish tost!

My love! thy parting smile
Will never reconcile
My life to such exile;
At such a cost!

I grudge thee not thy state;
But why did'st make me wait?
If of my cruel fate,
Thou certain wast!

To the Missionaries of Faith.*

Ye harbingers of love divine !
Inheritors of grace !

Bestow your efforts to refine
The fallen Indian race.

Once wanton Darkness here prevail'd,
In callous hearts and small ;
And empty Learning naught avail'd,
But strengthen'd mental thrall

* It hardly seems to be in the nature of things, that Christianity can gain on the subtle Indian intellect. As a race, we have little emotion or impulse in a matter like this ; and thus what is readily accepted by the more exquisitely nerved European, as the direct outcome of revelation, with us, sinks into a burst of pure fanaticism. *Faith*, which precedes and supersedes *thought* with the devout Christain, and which has been, from time to time, working magically on the most sublime intellects of the West, seldom actuates the heart of the proud Asiatic who strives to purchase salvation with *work*, and never stoops to accept it as alms, as it assuredly would be, if *faith* were to be his only merit. Still, it must be borne in mind, that all human work falls short in this, as in every other case. But I am drifting into speculations infinitely above my powers. I have only to add here, that missionary influence, in all other respects, has been the making of India ; for more than half of the spiritual and mental blessings we at present enjoy, are through the noble efforts of these children of God.

The haze of hesitating Doubt
Eclips'd the sun of Faith ;
The soul her vital fare without,
Once liv'd in moral Death.

For future weal, the soul's relief,
Was left no solid scope ;
The cankerworm of Unbelief
When sapp'd the tree of Hope.

The spring of Charity refus'd
Its life-breathing supply ;
For giant Selfishness then us'd
Its fountain shoal and dry.

From sire to son, foul Error's heirs,
Our lives undeck'd remain'd ;
That lamp of Love which Death out-stares,
In darkness wax'd and wan'd.

And thus midst sound apparent health,
A mighty system wheel'd ;
The core Corruption gnaw'd by stealth,
The body kept conceal'd.

Till, at catholic Love's behest,
And Sympathy's appeal,
Ye brought the unction of the West,
Our souls diseas'd to heal.

Midst thoughts incredulous and free,
With Superstitions rife,
Ye taught the blest economy
Of spiritual life.

The burst of light your advent grac'd
That flash'd on callous hearts,
Dispell'd their Doubt, and thus replac'd
In pristine glow their parts.

And Faith, emerging from the cloud,
An ample glory shed;
Oh may it its recipients proud
To life eternal wed!

The empty fountain of Good-will,
Replenish'd and alive,
Yields living waters, to the fill
To drink, and Death survive.

A verdant bow'r of Hope appears,
Before the human view ;
The troubl'd soul no longer fears
A wither'd avenue.
Oh may the Lord, His heralds gift
With martyr-strength and grace !
Away may scepticism drift,
At Persuasion's caress !
May all foretaste eternity,
The joys which it presents ;
May God in us erected see
'His Mercy's monuments' !

Time Alias Death.*

What worlds, condemn'd to thy mysterious womb,
Lie reeking in their blood, thou triumphant Time !
Thou'st brought unnumber'd lives to thy cold tomb.
And still with fatal force thy bell doth chime.
Drop, Drop weak human voice !
This Tyrant must rejoice.

* Suggested on reading Mrs. Heman's pathetic address to the Sea. 1868.

Thou wring'st maternal hearts, and stalwart sires,
Full anguish'd at their loss, bereft—forlorn—
Deplore their awful fate : their hope expires,
With rising hopes precarious, roughly torn, !
Thou blast, o'er-whelming blast !
How long thou'lt raging last ?

With stealthy steps thou gain'st thy hedious aim.
Exacting in thy choice, no bribe can buy
A truce with Time ! with hard impetuous claim,
Thou smothers't babes without a passing sigh.
Hold, hold thou drunken thief !
Why prey'st on breaths so brief ?

Thy quick career no earthly cause can tell.
No human force can stem thy jealous tide.
Thy poison'd winds, inflam'd, infectious swell.
Beneath them, gasping, thousand heroes hide.
Wait, wait thou flying pest !
Can none escape thy haste ?

Yes, those of sterling worth, and conscious faith,
Who ever wear sublime, unshrinking hearts,
Escape his sting. They scorn the threats of Death.
From them with down-cast looks the fiend departs.
Turn, turn thou baffl'd fool!
Dost seek promiscuous rule?

A Wreck of Humanity.*

Behold the wreck of a design,
Adroitly form'd and nobly wrought
By selfsame Architect divine,
That Plato form'd and Bacon taught.
Belike a suicide's picture sad,
The victim looks a living ghost;
His ghastly smiles, full often add
Fresh horrors to his features lost.
Each limb to him a traitor turns;
Each thought assumes a body foul;
His mind, no more, his pleasure learns,
But greets each action with a scowl.

* On the death of a notorious young profligate. 1869.

He bears the weight of early age ;
And his own converse seeks to shun ;
His thoughts eternal gloom presage ;
For dark Despair her end hath won.
O just from self, an exile sweet,
Or loss of ever-busy brain,
Would be to him a glorious treat—
To whom his life itself's a pain !
Thus hunted unto death, the wretch
Breathes on a rank sepulchral breath ;
A second step, a further stretch,
The vermin crawls, at last, to death !

Time of famine.

The Lord sits erect on His high throne of grace ;
And wrath righteous starts, in red flames, from His face.
A nation's neglect of His awful commands
Results in the ruin of the once happy land.
The scenes that the eye once with smiles did salute,
Bereft of their charms, wear a dark mourning suite.

The tall verdant trees that once whisper'd to Heav'n
Their thanks for the glorious inheritance giv'n,
Now bankrupt and bare, from their dwellings depart,
In nakedness vile to the cold venal mart.
The fields of their glory, no longer, can boast;
The wind for their plight doth them far and wide post.
The faint vegetation lies breathless and dry;
And some quarters it begs of the hot frowning sky.
The rich soil is turn'd to a desert of dirt;
And lives in its bosom lie cold and inert.
The Lord's heated breath all fresh waters have dried;
The land of its annual rain is denied.
The poison'd air carries diseases throughout;
Its effects discomfit hearts tender and stout.
The farmer runs wild, while his looks interpret
The fact that the foul reign of famine has set.
For weeks now he waits for his once daily pelf;
And prays to his gods, more inane than himself!

The folly of War.*

These bloody pictures, scenes so sad,
Unseemly envy, fury mad,
This wild impulse of rude Caprice,
This vaulting rage of Avarice,
I blush to see them grow, my God!
And Health and Youth by War down-trod.
Yon guns and swords, malignant things,
Yon cannons, muskets, ruthless kings!
Why use you them, ye regal fools!
Ambition's slaves, ye passion's tools?
Demand ye more than gifts divine?*
Should sin-born man for further pine?
Were they not kings, who liv'd and died
Possess'd of much, more satisfied?
Should Monarchs' anger Kingdoms stir?
Should Might the strength of Right aver?
No, child of Greed! if life's a span,
If sorry worm is all that's man,

* 1872.

If bliss above thy aim be sole,
Than earthly pomp and wide control,
On God, if future weal depend,
And dying safe be living's end,
This passion shun! Let Nations' joy
Thy first, thy earnest thoughts employ.
Let not the brother-tie be torn—
Thus save thy kind from woes unborn. !

An ode to Night.

Sweet Night! my brief and rare recess!
Protract, in mercy's name, thy flight.
O why dost thou so swift progress?
Be not o'er-jealous of thy right.
Imperfect death,—unconscious life—
Refreshing bath for Mind's relief—
Armistice of diurnal strife—
The busy workman's solace brief—
The groaning patient's rich-bought health—
The honey-moon of revelry—

The earnest of the student's wealth
For future gain—are lodg'd in thee!
Dream-store of youth, still, solemn time!
Delicious for celestial search;
When I, Creation's charms sublime,
Examine, from my lonesome perch.
O Night! my charitable friend!
To me a longer leisure yield,
To court my Muse. If thou descend,
Day drags me to life's battle-field.

The British character. *

Brave Isle! what rugged life is thine,
E'er rocking on Oceania's breast!
And yet thy sons and daughters shine,
The pride and charm of modern West!
How proudly true, how nobly fair
The children that belong to Thee!
Where Work is lov'd and Wisdom rare;
Where Learning spreads her canopy.

* 1870.

Where Indolence, a vice is held, ;
Where Caste and Custom never thrive ;
Where Freedom, by deep Faith impell'd,
Keeps Thought and Action e'er alive !
By nature true, they 're prompt and bold,
While rock'd in cradle, country-proud ;
The widow's stay, the orphan's hold,
The tyrant's constant foes avow'd !
To them the Main's no mistery ;
Their minds have reach'd the Firmament.
Them mighty Mounts teach history ;
And Sand and Stone a life present !
They care to live, they dare to die,
They live to learn ; and last they leave
Their works, that Nature's ire defy :
They work, and in their might believe !

A career of Crime.

Stern majesty adorns his brow,
Grim vengeance sweeps his port,
As swift, the glance of Khanderow *
Pursues the crouching court.

When, choak'd with rage, he looks around,
His nostrils fire emit ;
His eyeballs from their sockets bound ;
His lips look purpose-knit.

The courtiers tremble, aspen-like !
The minions look askance ;
His movements those with horror strike,
These check in servile dance.

The nervous, restless starts betray
His secret counsels dark ;
The absent looks, that speech delay,
Some mental conflict mark.

* Khanderow, the tenth Gaicowar, a brave and munificent prince, altogether unlike that atrocious idiot Malarow, his brother and successor.

A haggard look arrests his view,
Whom mortal terrors scare ;
His eyes, o'er-spread with ashy hue,
Wild apprehension stare !

The traitor-brother stands before ;
Detested far and wide ;
E'er thirsty for some kindred gore—
A would-be fratricide.

The craven craves his life with tears,
In contrite tones and hoarse ;
And then to ties of blood adheres—
The coward's last resource.

'Oh' cries the bursting injur'd heart,
In tones of helpless force,
'Oh Why doth cruel Nature thwart'
'Just Retribution's course ?'

'Thou wretch ingrate ! if from their rest,'
'The shades of all our sires'—
'A spectral train, did me request'
'To save thee from hell-fires'—

'Did all the world her eloquence',
'In thy defence engage';
'Too weak that advocate's defence'
'Would be to calm my rage'—

'Or if the gods, with bribes well-wrought,'
'Of partnership divine',
'On bended knees, thy safety sought';
'The offer I'd decline'.

'No wretch! in thought and action mean';
'In deadly treasons rife';
'By no reward would I have been'
'Trick'd of thy carrion life'.

'But though I can't take life, with joy,'
'Life's charm I take away';
'Go, live, but life for e'er employ'
'The hire of crime to pay'.

'And if this news, to thy dead sense',
'A ray of comfort sends',
'For triumph thou hast no pretence,'
'Though 'scaping Vengeance' ends'.

When at the end of this decree,
Assurance was restor'd,
The culprit stood, from death tho' free,
By Love and Faith ignor'd.

His will express'd, the king reclin'd,
By diverse passions sway'd;
To make it law, with haste unkind,
His Nemesis obey'd.

For fallen greatness few can feel;
And fewer thoughts express;
For pity men at premium deal,
In trouble or distress.

The lost intriguer's vile estate,
Is touching sore to see—
His quaking form, crush'd with its weight,
Convuls'd in agony!

A wild unearthly cry is heard,
In hollow tones and weird;
That curse of life he's now incurr'd,
Which most of all he fear'd!

A sick'ning dream his sense o'er-pow'rs;
In vision he perceives
Some Retribution-guarded tow'rs,
Some cords his fancy weaves !

Grim tortures greet his guilt-stain'd view,
And anguish-tears compell;
Some dungean dark exhumes anew,
Its tainted poison-cell.

The past his reason's vitals drinks;
And stripp'd of sense, he raves;
For mental balance crumbling sinks
'Neath Mem'ry's rushing waves.

* * *

The scene is chang'd, the victor bold,
A victim's in his turn;
The lord of lands he could not hold,
Can scarce fill up an urn!

The voice that thunder-claps out-vied,
In loftiness of tones,
Is now the pow'r of pray'r denied;
And at the effort moans !

The sinew'd arms, two ready slaves
Of will that none could check,
Now helpless lie in lethal waves—
Two sails of human wreck!

The lively glance that war conveyed,
In every movement stray,
The gen'ral slumber now obeyed,
And in truce eternal lay!

The news runs with the fleeting blast,
At wondrous rapid rate;
The town it travels; then at last,
Knocks at a prison-gate.

'Thrice welcome nymph,' a heart exclaims,
From light and joy exil'd;
'At last in Hope's delicious realms,'
'Thou hast my soul beguil'd'!

A change undreamt of sudden floats
Upon the waves of time,
Which in its headlong course pro mos
A mad career of crime.

The prison-gates are flung apart;
And many a smile and bow,
Of instant birth, begot of art,
Their honesty avow.

The woe-worn form in silk they dress,
Emboss'd with burning gold;
His head the rarest gems caress,
Most beauteous to behold.

They kneel to him in homage mute—
The mean and servile band;
And with their loyal lips salute
His lank and sin-stain'd hand!

And thus they see him on the throne;
And pray to him for peace;
Well might they ask the storms that groan,
To spare the virgin breeze!

Confirm'd in habits reprobate,
Congenial to his tastes,
The remnant of his manly state,
In lewdness now he wastes.

An epicure, to pleasures prone,
Of homicidal bent,
On gentle blood and pure alone,
The monster is intent.

A universal death his goal,
Each loss to him is gain;
For once was his detested soul
Sold to the sin of Cain.*

His fatal aim he basely sets
On Beauty and on Worth;
The sight of that his lust begets,
The ruin of this his mirth.

Truth, Honesty and Virtue are
His heart's aversion strong;
And all his actions foul refer
To cruel private wrong.

Till Youth and Worth and Virtue find
Some more congenial haunt;

About, 1867 he was found very busy trying to compass his brother's death.

And safe, though selfish, leave behind
Black Vice and Age and Want.

Till mad Impatience trac'd these woes,
To Heav'n's complying hand;
Forgetful that the Lord but knows
To *prosper* every land!

But He Whose comprehensive care
Extends to *insect* birth;
Will He, in such a strait forswear
His images on earth?

The driv'ling gamester who could stake
His soul on many a chance,
Too late perceives his glory's wreck,
When waking from the trance!

His eyeballs piteously distend;
Sad looks his state forlorn,
When for his own, a foreign friend
Begs *he*—a monarch born!

To tear-pledg'd words and bended knees,
No further heed is lent:

Too dear is held the millions' peace,
For fresh experiment.

Thus dead in life, forgotten lies,
Unhappy Malarow ;*
The widow's wails, the orphan's cries
His soul no rest allow !

In bitter grief, the wretch we see
Spin out his earthly span ;
'Forget' says human charity,
'Earth once held such a man' !

---

* The life of this man presents a strange anomaly. Though a total imbecile, he seemed to take exquisite delight in every luxury of torture that revenge or malice could suggest. He has of late been whimpering from time to time, that the political pill Lord Northbrook made him swallow, was too big and too bitter. Perhaps it *was* so. But 'the end justifies the means'. As for himself, our late Viceroy has left behind, a lasting memorial of his wisdom and justice for the grateful admiration of posterity.

A Protest.*

Does not a foreign and invidious rack,
Out here in India, break poor Labour's back?
Is not our Skill, adorn'd with sterling worth,
Condemn'd unseen, because of *Indian* birth?
Does not Conceit our conscious Strength deride?
And call it Weakness, with unblushing pride?
But right of Conquest is not stinted still:
Our lives are forfeit at the stranger's will!
We heard, erewhile, of Fuller masterful:
How well he knows his heathen slaves to rule!
Is Rámá idle? Kicks and cuffs must cure
That heinous crime, which law can ne'er endure!
One day the Saheb, in his lordly style,
Some orders issues to the syce senile.

* Mr. Fuller's apologists might not relish these lines; but they would do well to reflect whether the learned Vakeel was under any circumstances justified in behaving as he did. It is one thing to sympathize with an awkwardly-placed friend; and another to hold him up as a mirror of manliness, simply because he happened to have animal strength enough to kick a poor bed-rid Bengali out of existence!

Now sick of spleen, the syce o'er-sleeps the hour,
And puts his carcass in vex'd Virtue's pow'r.
The household stands in mute unbroken awe,
As he drags the culprit from his bed of straw.
In breathless rage, hot kicks he lays about,
Till footsore nature can no more hold out.
Then shakes that frame of dry disjointed bones;
And flings him ruthless, midst his bitter groans!
The victim reels, each limb in mortal siege,
From reckless force, to 'scape fresh sacrilege.
'What? run when punish'd?, the Saheb's heard to yell';
'Is that the way, my righteous wrath to quell?'
'I'll teach ye manners'; and with murd'rous breath,
The wretch he chases to a certain death!
Plump drops the syce! but ere the lord relents,
A friendly swoon his instant death prevents!
The timid wife—her woman's soul astir,
Against this conduct breathes a faint demur.
'For the Lord's love, my dear, some doctor search,'
'Oh h——g the Lord! will you now go to Church?'
A man of church, each Sabbath he attends
The house of God, and there in prayer bends!

The mild divine his flock to love exhorts—
Such love as e'en all scorn and hatred courts.
Then charm'd with th' audience all-absorbèd gaze,
His soul's glad tribute on the altar lays.
His pious lips a grateful pray'r absorbs:
And the tear of peace steals down his agèd orbs.
What kens the guileless sire, of our hero's sin?
His warm responses straight his friendship win!
Long kneels he there, the grace of Heav'n to seek,
For all the errors of the bygone week!
Then light of heart, he homeward wends his way,
In *peace* and *love* to spend the blessèd day!
But now his guilt, its effects dread unfolds,
And the lifeless syce, his trembling lord beholds!
The court assembles, where strange lights they glean—
The syce was suff'ring from a *ruptur'd spleen!*
All deeply weigh'd, the court impartial says,
That *two pounds* English can such lives purchase!
Thus died the syce, to splenic mem'ry link'd,
And the world sang praises, as His Worship wink'd!

A soul despatch'd, in nudeness and in woe,
To glooms eternal, in the shades below!
Rash Guilt, excus'd by pamper'd Prejudice,
Erewhile goes free, and thanks the law remiss.
But fix'd as fate, and quick as crime conceiv'd,
Alights fair Justice, in her heart aggriev'd.
At first she falters; but a herald brave,
With words of welcome, doth her advent pave.
His Daniel's soul, thro' birth and breed has worn,
A range unbounded and a godly turn.
Thus walks the maid of sempiternal youth,
'Tween Christian candour and celestial truth.
Hail virgin goddess! Heav'n-affianc'd bride
Of British Honor, Britain's noblest pride!
Faith's glorious first-born! in all fairness giv'n,
To lend the righteous firmer hold on Heav'n!
Hail beauteous pow'r! long-ancestor'd maid!
Whom Perse and Israel pristine homage paid!
Whom Greece and Rome and hoary Egypt knew!
And from whose presence, Ind her splendour drew!
Hail proud Justitia! stern, unerring grace!
Thou ancient heirloom of the Aryan race!

Best friend to Order and to spirit free,
All hail thou soul of sacred majesty ! !
So Justice came ; and to the world proclaim'd,
That black or white, she was for either fram'd—
That Law has meaning of no stinted breadth ;
That death it hates, tho' 'tis a heathen's death.
The syce is dead : beyond all troubles hurl'd,
Of a sad existence in a weary world ! .
How feels his lord ? Has he the sight forgot,
Of death and anguish, by his passion wraught ?
Do not pale fancies and grim shadows wan,
His vision haunting, scare the inner man ?
Does not he weep, what time two pleading eyes
Remind the tyrant of th' expiring syce ?
Does not he tremble, midst his safest joys,
When hush'd he hears the faint imploring voice ?
Be that his scourge ! enough, if in his breast,
He feels his guilt—the guilt of heartless haste.
To Heav'n he's false; and false to nature most,
If of this guilt, he makes a wanton boast !

Genius in Power.

How sweet is life, where Genius sways
A nation's destiny!
And spies their wants, thro' lucent rays
Of hallow'd Sympathy!

The child of Woe, when on her knees,
She lulls to balmy rest,
With cordials of sweet lullabies,
In tones of love addrest!

The ire-knit brow when checks the freak
Of wanton Wilfulness;
And shields the struggling and tho weak,
From Tyrann'ys excess!

Whose ear or eye fair Virtue's tale,
When patient hears or reads,
As trembling with anxiety pale,
Deep Love or Pity pleads!

When stern in love, in justice meek,
She banishes Offence,

His sin-bound soul's relief to seek,
In dreary penitence !

When Genius, (twin-born of true Pow'r)
Thus manifests her worth,
The land appears an angel's dow'r—
A faultless Heav'n on earth ! *

To the Disloyal Grumbler.

Oh mourn thou not in vain regrets,
That fanci'd wrongs thy peace alloys,
When thy ungrateful heart forgets
What bliss thy conquer'd race enjoys !
What if thy English brother lords
It o'er thee, with contempt impli'd ?
Recall the day when Moslem swords
Cut thee and thine in wanton pride !
Think how a gen'rous nation strives,
To win thee back thy prestige lost !

* And such, India undoubtedly would be, if each Viceroy were a Lytton, each General a Havelock, and each Missionary a Wilson.

Of what dear joys, herself deprives,
To aid thee at a frightful cost!
I see the wife, with trembling hands,
Her parting hero's kerchief weave;
Knows she that climate's cold demands,
Erelong will her of peace berieve?
I see the mother's idol spread
His arms for the, the last embrace;
He knows—she too has faintly read,—
These tears but sadder scenes preface!
I see the gallant soldier tear,
From hearth and home, his manhood's prize;
O think, but think how well she bears
Her hard, her life-long sacrifice!
And where's the husband, young and hale?
Go 'gainst the sword or sun exclaim;
To *him* thy grief's of small avail:
The wife's a widow all the same!
And where's the joyless widow's joy?
Ask yonder mocking shades and gaunt;
Strange sights now with her fancy toy;
And visions sad her mem'ry haunt!

But where's that timid trust-bound heart, *
That long inspir'd the patriot brave ?
List, grumbler list, and do not start,
That heart hath grac'd a foreign grave !
When thoughts of this my senses crowd,
Good God ! my nerves are all unstrung ;

* One day, amusing an idle hour with a local calendar, my eyes lighted on the following modest, and therefore, touching obituary :—Died at Genoa——wife of———.Knowing the husband to be then living in Bombay, I indulged in a train of the most melancholy reverie:——— The poor delicate being, hastening home from an oppressive sun; alone— because the husband must remain behind to earn the wherewithal to defray the expenses of a long journey; taking the separation to heart ——unconscious that shortly after, she would doom him to a much longer separation ; denying herself these little luxuries, needed for her sex and her situation—that he might not be worried; and then perhaps, coming to an untimely end ; perhaps too, without a friend to bear her dying blessing to him for whom she had lived ! Can India ever repay the bereaved husband his loss ? Instances like this are not rare of occurrence. Many must have heard of the death of poor W. H. Havelock. Going home to recruit health, shattered by over-exertion ; snatching, as if it were, a few hasty draughts of pure English air ; coming out again in a hardly convalescent state ; rushing madly to the help of the famine-stricken people ; falling a victim to his own impetuous generosity ; and thus robbing the Government of an invaluable servant, and the people of a trusted and esteemed friend ! What a bright and hopeful life was his ! How sad and dreary of the poor wife and orphans !

Hot tears of shame my vision shroud,
And tears by grateful pity wrung.
And none, with common souls with mine,
But feels his patriot's sense profan'd;
If, yielding to the morbid whine,
One prates of 'rights and pow'rs restrain'd'.
From motives int'rested apart,
As guardian of our peace and pride,
In every honest British heart,
I hail my brother, friend and guide!
And though my heart, my head, my hand,
My country's welfare holds in pawn,
Still more I owe to that brave land,
From whom alone that welfare's drawn.
Glad land of proud heroic pow'r!
It were but carrion blood that curb'd
Its gen'rous flow, at that dread hour,
When thy bright lustre's least disturb'd.
Then cheap-bought I'd thy safety hold,
If life and lucre were its price;
And joys I'd feel, unfelt, untold,
On listening to my heart's advice!

Till then, as oft as to her God,
My soul her homage sweet conveys,
Of naught my country, she'll defraud,
With her for Britain if she prays.
And grateful to the Father's ear,
Will be that suit unselfish, fair;
And His bright smile glad Ind shall cheer,
In answer to a patriot's pray'r!

A Sketch.

When never fond a friend or foe to bore,
You ask me, why I pen this brief memoir?
In sooth, sir reader! 'tis to swell the book—
No easy task—so doff that curious look!
Five years before the Queen wore India's crown,
I saw the light of hot Baroda town.
And ere three years, untoward mischief marr'd
My parents' peace, and union fresh debarr'd.
We left our sire. A waggon stock'd with hay,
In that dread journey, kept the Bheels * at bay.

* A race of highway robbers in Gujarat, now almost extinct, thanks to the British rule.

None could describe my mother's patience brave,
As we cross'd the crisis in that grassy grave.
How slow we sped! however, every while,
We thank'd our God, each hour we trudg'd a mile!
At last we reach'd fair Surat's ancient walls,
When my mother hasten'd to th' ancestral halls.
Not hers those halls; soon as her claim she set,
Rude strangers' gaze her fond advances met.
Poor ill-starr'd mother! dear hopeful soul!
Those mem'ries sad my life's best joys control!
Though scant her store, by chance capricious left,
Long made she last it, with her fingers deft.
Thus humbly blest, I spent the first six years
Of my checker'd life, in smiles unmix'd with tears.
Life then a light and lasting frolic seem'd,
Each idle hour, with freshborn joys redeem'd.
High time 'twas thought, now in my heart to breed
Some pious notions of Zoroaster's creed.
A likely man they found, a weaver * wise,

* It was a common practice among the Parsis to entrust their children to Mobeds, who while working at the loom, gave them oral lessons in the sacred writings of Zoroaster.

Advanc'd in years, and moral exercise.
White flowing beard, small chirping voice,
White white his all, but red his blinking eyes!
A man mysterious of the Magus tribe—
A close astrologer, and a splendid scribe—
A faithful oracle of dread Hormazd's will—
A priest, a patriarch, and a man of skill.
A master weaver, and—to close details—
He weav'd long webs, and Lord! he weav'd long tales!
Hard murd'rous words, that wisdom's lips defied,
Would thick portentous from his nozzle glide!
And here we stuck, tho' long and hard we tried;
He curs'd, and can'd by turns, we humm'd and cried!
This could not last; our mutual failings seen,
He left his preaching and we left our dean.
From him releas'd, I found myself transferr'd
To one by housewives, nam'd the 'urchin-herd'.*

* A very ungodly looking man of God, and the terror of all city-imps and street-arabs.

A zealous man he was, a man of parts,
With scanty science, but a host of *arts.*
With pointed paws his fierce mustache he'd twirl,
And at the culprits the direst vengeance hurl.
His jaws he'd rub, his grizzl'd beard peck,
Till rubb'd and peck'd, the whole appear'd a wreck.
Which in a polish'd glass, he then would quiz,
And look complacent at his mottl'd phiz!
A wag by nature and a stoic sour,
'Tis hard to fix his equivocal pow'r.
Good cheer he lov'd, and oft a dainty dish
His wrath diverted as we well could wish.
When thus begorg'd, joy, joy was all his work!
His air all blandness, and his face all smirk!
But woe betide the hour, if e'er his meal
Was late; that would his hidden traits reveal.
His zeal rose higher, as his stomach fell;
And hard his fervour on our skins would tell!
Sharp went the whizzing whip, fast flew the cane;
And he fairly caper'd in his wrath insane!

He chanted pray'rs, oh Lord! in such gruff tones,
'Twould set on rack the hoar Zoroaster's bones!
Then came his comments, cook'd with such abuse,
As would a Rabelais' gross sense confuse!
He shriek'd and stagger'd in his zealous rage,
Till he look'd an actor on a tragic stage!
And when our whines, the neighb'ring women drew,
The man of zeal, at once persuasive grew!
Expounded doctrines, in a fervid breath,
Preach'd *patience, virtue, truth and tacit faith*!
Thank God, I'd then too small religious wit,
To understand that canting hypocrite.
Now times were chang'd; we lost our little all;
But bore with patience, lank Penury's thrall.
At nine I learnt my ways and means to judge—
A sage precocious and a driftless drudge.
'Twas then a bootless gipsy life I led;
My food dry biscuits and chill stones my bed.
One suite of cottons, all the worse for wear,
My carcass shelter'd from skies foul or fair.

A hybrid cap, of known and unknown hues,
Fresh rescued from some box, of rags profuse—
A threadbare shirt, the wreck of jackets loose,
Past e'en a cold and callous miser's use—
Ill-sorted breeches, in all freedom free,
That tried to look their vain apology—
And shoes that would a clumsy cobbler fright,
By their shape nondescript and their shrunken sight.
And oft bedeck'd in such a gallant gear,
I homage drew in both my front and rear!
But friends, still loath to see me gather wool,
Once more decreed that I should go to school.

A seedy Brahmin, with a visage stern,
Was the lord despotic of this new concern.
His speech tho' scant, such as calm peace portends,
His hands and feet for that made full amends.
For kicks and cuffs his favourite pastime form'd,
Unlike his race, he *rain'd* but seldom *storm'd!*
And now a change, a during change was wraught,
That strangely work'd upon my future lot.

The only being I ador'd on earth,
The joy and solace of my mundane birth,
Whose one fond smile my life's long sunshine spread,
And whose one sad tear was my constant dread,—
My angel mother, in ripe youth was ta'en,
By some foul disorder to her bed of pain.
This rescu'd me from habits chronic grown,
Of vagrant life, to settl'd state unknown.
One thought my new-awaken'd mind possess'd,
To nurse my parent and her health revest.
Three slow-sped years, I watch'd her bed of care,
By day and night her vigils long to share.
But still a son's devout and soul-sprung pray'r,
Could not with Heav'n prevail, her life to spare.
One day the sun as his decline began,
Declin'd the sun of this my earthly span!
Her latest breath below my safety sought—
To bless her orphan was her dying thought!
No tear I shed, when first my loss I view'd:
My sense was smother'd and my soul subdu'd.

She'd clasp'd a child, with sad emotions wan ;
But when the clasp relax'd, there was left a man.
A man at twelve ! in whom my grief confide ?
No friend to watch me but the sainted guide !
And when this thought upon my reason stole,
A sudden desolation o'er-spread my soul !
Now sober grown, my mind to study turn'd ;
And thus impell'd, I fresh to school adjourn'd.
God bless my teacher ! * who with pious love,
My thoughts directed to bright hopes above.
His massive forehead, and his pensive brows—
And face sedate, that peace with God avows—
His look benign, that none could e'er displease—
The faithful emblem of a soul at ease—
His honey'd accents that each other chas'd
In swift succession—these my wonder rais'd.
His zeal was catching, and by its large supply,
My thoughts expanded and my soul soar'd high.
Book after book, my frenzi'd longing fed ;
For English lore a boundless field displayed.

* The late Rev. William Dixon, M. A.

At six and ten, with heaps of embroy rhymes,
I took my passage to more genial climes.
Two pounds I borrow'd, at a frightful rate,
To make the journey in a fitting state !
And when a wardrobe and some books purchased,
Ten shillings odd was all my pockets grac'd !
Still men were kind ; and tho' my mission fail'd,
Their friendship cool'd not, nor their malice rail'd.
But partial Fortune, that malicious witch,
Has e'er since doom'd me to a life of switch !
'Twas hard indeed, to train crude unform'd brains,
To rigid methods and sententious strains.
Boys first rebell'd ; but all their ridicule
Ceas'd at the flourish of my crisp ferule !
Ye gods of grammar ! how at first they talk'd,
Each part of speech at rules grammatic mock'd !
They read in tones such as would make one stare,
Till he caught their tones and wept in sheer despair !
They scrawl'd such pothooks, one could sooner read
The grim hieroglyphs of Egyptian breed !

For months I suffer'd, with a martyr's grace,
The wanton vagaries of this urchin race.
At last a key I found, a master key,
That soft as oil unlock'd the mystery.
A stock of patience, by each strain unmov'd,
Is the golden secret of this art approv'd.
And next, to have abundant sympathy,
For faults and foibles from which none are free—
To smile and frown alternate, all around,
Throughout the task to keep a lull profound—
The dull to quicken and the stiff to bend,
And to the erring one a hand extend—
To censure many and to praise but few,
The weak to strengthen, and the strong subdue.
This system follow'd, future troubles sav'd;
And peace prevailing, high her banner wav'd.
But now when leisure, by good chance, I earn'd,
My trick of scribbling in full blush return'd.
To which I yielded, and on a friendly hint,
Regal'd the public with some lines in print.

A clique of critics, each a jobbernowl,
From a novel standard, of this book fell foul.
'This bit of man', cried one, in scorn supreme,
'Who wears no glasses, and who rides no whim',
'Who reads not Reynolds, and who shuns the stage',
'Can he write books, in this enlighten'd age' ?
Straight ran the champion of the public taste;
And call'd a council of detractors chaste.
But the world was wiser, and our gallant goose
Had to read his judgments to his friend the deuce.
They scandal spread—he and his scurvy crews;
And sought my *death* with *mortal* long reviews.
In this when balk'd, they nameless letters wrote,
My ruin retailing by an adverse vote.
They made me *shake*, whene'er by *ague* smit;
And then they triumph'd, ah! how hard they hit!
By *nights* I fasted from a guilty sense,
My *days* went sleepless and in toil intense!
But life outliv'd this curious regimen,
My heart unbroken, and unspent my pen.

And thus at twenty-two, I scan the world,
Its valves of folly and of crime unfurl'd.
Though toss'd and tumbl'd on its fickle waves,
One fact Experience on my heart engraves—
Its wrongs and rancour we can swim above,
If our rule of life be universal love.
Let grim Satire break her noisome jaws,
'Twill give us relish for a friend's applause.
If jaundic'd Envy opes her poison'd throat,
In conscious pow'r, we have an antidote.
The soul, when thus to mild forbearance train'd,
Will live in peace, by troubles unprofan'd.
And own 'tis worthier 'bove its ills to soar,
Than call life a curse, and wish to live no more!

My first grief.

The solar reign is ended nigh;
The stars are peeping thro' the sky;
Sweet Eve is in a sombre dye
Attiring.

There lies a form in Death's domain,
Whose eyes a show'r of tears rain—
Sad hostages to Want and Pain
Conspiring.

Two wistful eyes, sad witnesses,
The pathos of the scene increase,
This trouble's cause, on bended knees
Inquiring.

Two wan lips bid a farewell smile,
The mourner's first grief to beguile ;
The smiler though lies all the while
Expiring.

Sad yearning looks, in anguish drest,
Now with anxiety's gloom invest
The spirit to her final rest
Retiring.

The suff'rer ends her earthly stroll ;
The witness yet his course doth roll ;
Bright hopes of union e'er his soul
Inspiring.

To the genius of the Bard of Rydal.

With shallow sense, a world of wit obtuse,
Mispriz'd my Wordsworth's chaste tho' mystic muse.
Where heavy Art commanded praise unwise,
Free Nature's flow was found a strange surprise.
Chamelion-like when Byron's genius shone—
A dapple iris, by Narcisus * drawn ;
When fever'd Frenzy sought the Paphian skies,
On cloying sense to feast her morbid eyes;

* If ever a mortal resembled the beautiful son of Cephisus, it was Lord Byron—too beautiful and too egotistic withal, to retain any clear appreciation of the glories of a vast creation around him. In the midst of the most intoxicating public attention, his restless spirit flitted from spot to spot, in search of a higher and more ideal happiness; and when experience whispered to him the futility of his errand, he peevishly fell back upon himself. This self-worship served him but as an opiate; and in the intervals of consciousness, the man felt that his better nature was evaporating, drop by drop; and that to prevent the utter destruction of his soul, he needed the sympathy of his kind. But what, appeal to the sympathy of those whom he had dazzled with the eloquence of his scornful genius? He would none of it! Such was the troubled career of this self-bewitched genius!

In Pleasure's lap, when thus by Fashion lull'd,
The British soul felt enervate and dull'd ;
Like new-born sun, in sober strength he swept
His country's shame ; and in Nature's ways adept,
And conscious of a high and inborn grace,
On Truth and Nature shed his magic rays !
Loud were the sneers, and strong the scorn he brav'd ;
But ne'er his heart his glorious birthright wav'd !
To me, sweet Bard ! thy page rare light dictates,
As on my soul thy music verse vibrates.
Thy power seems, in every subtile shade,
A later offspring of sage Zarthost's * head.

* It is a significant fact, that though more than thirty centuries have rolled over the age of Zoroaster; and though a hundred nations have had their rise and their fall since then; his religion stands, almost in its pristine simplicity, a monument to the lofty genius of its founder. Whenever my mind attempts to peep 'into the fathomless past', the spirit of the prophet, poet and philosopher of Persia, strikes it with speechless awe. His poetry is not the poetry of the wild enthusiast—there is no exhibition of fierce human passions, no revolting pictures of after-horrors there. It is the poetry of nature—deep, solemn, meditative poetry—teaching the soul to hold an almost visible communion with her Maker. Nor is his philosophy, the cold shadowy brain-bauble of the sceptic—it is cheerful and heart-enlivening, having 'good thought, good word and good deed' as the three stepping stones to Heaven. And on this striking combination of poetry and philosophy, his genius sheds the mystic light of prophecy.

Thus it is that we see him, adorning a remote antiquity with his divine presence, and standing, in conscious dignity, the observed of a million observers, bursting with wild 'acclamations to the echo of his name'.

'Tween him and thee, a common soul I trace,
The same vast genius, but in time and place.
The same rich judgment in a modest word,
In one like line, the same deep truth unheard.
The same life's views, the same Heav'n-seeking aim,
The same your taste, your worth and work the same.
Of each, with equal awe, I trembling sing:
Each mighty mind as Nature's heir and king!

To the glorious West.

Hail beauteous view of far Columbian soil,
Where rich and poor, for common progress toil;
Where rigid patriots 'gainst their parent hurled
Defiant force, to save their virgin world;
Reviv'd and rais'd, beneath th' etherial dome,
Where Earth once more beholds Republic Rome;
In all her wealth of Truth and Virtue hale,
And all her wisdom on a grander scale—
In all her warmth of patriotic fire,
Which thoughts unselfish of pure love inspire—

In all her pow'rs, immensely amplified,
Which Time and Fate, with scorn supreme deride—
Where Freedom-born, heroic Thought pursues
Imbecile Dogma and devout Abuse ;
Hail Nature's pride ! high Heav'n's maturest gift !
Thou glad asylum of the bold and swift !
A boundless distance tho' my heart o'erwhelms,
She wafts her blessings to thy prosp'rous realms.
Oh may they light on each deserving head—
The sire, the matron, and the youth and maid !

Defence of Time.

Upwards and onwards my brethren proceed,
In the solemn and still march of Time ;
The tempting repose you espy, do not heed ;
'Tis found in a far during clime.
The Earth's empty wages let soldiers accept,
Whose souls can no higher ascend ;
Too heavy their flight, of all motion bereft,
Their way towards Heaven to wend.

But let *us*, in this brief but decisive campaign,
Miss never *one* purpose sublime;
Eternity's shore 'tis that purpose to gain;
But that's thro' the channel of *Time*!
'Tis wicked and vain against Time to complain;
No stranger nor tyrant is he:
The first-born of Heav'n, in its boundless domain—
The earnest of Eternity!

The guide of my youth.

I had a friend whom Fancy need no brighter colours lend:
His genius was to love his race, his mission to befriend!
O how his magic smile beguil'd my dreary orphan lot!
But Fate dispell'd my dream, alas! He was, and he is not!
The world was dull and selfish; and malign all that to crown;
And my slighted youth was learning fast to offer frown for frown;

When lo! the light of Friendship true, upon my vision shot;
But short-liv'd were her genial joys; he was, and he is not!
His soul, like yonder sun in Heav'n, her wealth of light diffus'd,
On spirits that were good or evil—the blooming or the bruis'd!
Wo, wo is them! for whom the brave and hoary champion fought!
The fight of Faith is ended; for he was, and he is not!
Will not his counsel, steep'd in grace, my youth again rejoice?
O for those honey'd honey'd accents! O the nectar'd voice!
What then? Asleep, awake, have I a phantom idol sought?
'Yes', whispers cruel Past, 'because he was, but he is not'!

Manhood's dream.

'To glory or the grave'; Campbell.

O life is but a stagnant sea, a weary trackless main;
Its waves asphaltic undisturb'd, the soul with poison stain.
The glory of good work it is our better part can save;
I'll rush to glory deathless, then—to glory or the grave!
The ice of silence will the soul to selfish langour freeze!
While mine is yearning for some work of merit here she sees.
So fly to works of charity and love, my spirit brave!
To glory bear me on thy wings—to glory or the grave!
There's Pleasure luring me to ruin; I'll ne'er the siren heed;
If once my soul is wreck'd, she's naught but shame to wed indeed!
But no! I'd honest death prefer to being Pleasure's knave;
So up and on to glory, soul!—to glory or the grave!